DATE DUE

1948	

PRINTED IN U.S.A.

The United States

South Dakota

Anne Welsbacher
ABDO & Daughters

visit us at
www.abdopub.com

Published by Abdo & Daughters, 4940 Viking Drive, Suite 622, Edina, Minnesota 55435.
Copyright © 1998 by Abdo Consulting Group, Inc., Pentagon Tower, P.O. Box 36036,
Minneapolis, Minnesota 55435 USA. International copyrights reserved in all countries.
No part of this book may be reproduced in any form without written permission from the
publisher.

Printed in the United States.

Cover and Interior Photo credits: Archive, AP/Wide World, SuperStock, Peter Arnold, Inc.

Edited by Lori Kinstad Pupeza
Contributing editor Brooke Henderson
Special thanks to our Checkerboard Kids—Matthew Nichols, Stephanie McKenna,
Jack Ward

All statistics taken from the 1990 census; The Rand McNally Discovery Atlas of The
United States.

Library of Congress Cataloging-in-Publication Data

Welsbacher, Anne, 1955-
        South Dakota / Anne Welsbacher.
        p.   cm. -- (United States)
        Includes index.
        Summary: A brief introduction to the geography, history, natural resources,
        industries, cities, and people of the Mt. Rushmore State, South Dakota.
        ISBN 1-56239-898-9
        1. South Dakota--Juvenile literature. [1. South Dakota.] I. Title. II. Series:
        United States (Series)
        F651.3.W45   1998
        978.3--dc21   97-40695
                                                                         CIP
                                                                         AC

Contents

Welcome to South Dakota

South Dakota is called the Mount Rushmore State. The faces of four United States presidents are carved into the side of a bluff at Mount Rushmore. The high cliffs of the Black Hills are in South Dakota. The rugged **Badlands** are also in South Dakota.

Because of the sun and its rich land, farms cover much of South Dakota, and many South Dakotans are farmers.

Many Native American heroes lived in South Dakota. Chief Red Cloud fought to keep his land from being taken away. Today, people can still enjoy the pretty landscape as it was in Red Cloud's day.

Opposite page: Mount Rushmore, South Dakota.

Fast Facts

SOUTH DAKOTA

Capital
Pierre (12,906 people)
Area
75,956 square miles
(196,725 sq km)
Population
699,999 people
Rank: 45th
Statehood
November 2, 1889
(40th state admitted)
Principal rivers
James River
Missouri River
Highest point
Harney Peak;
7,242 feet (2,207 m)
Largest city
Sioux Falls (100,814 people)
Motto
Under God the people rule
Song
"Hail, South Dakota"
Famous People
Sitting Bull, Pierre Chouteau, Jr.,
Crazy Horse, Calamity Jane,
George McGovern, Laura Ingalls
Wilder

*S*tate Flag

*P*asque Flower

*R*ing-necked
Pheasant

*B*lack Hills Spruce

About South Dakota

The Mount Rushmore State

Detail area

SD

South Dakota's
abbreviation

Borders: west (Wyoming, Montana), north (North Dakota), east (Minnesota, Iowa), south (Nebraska)

Nature's Treasures

South Dakota has much rich soil. It is good for farming. Western South Dakota has grass-covered plains that make good grazing lands for cows.

The Black Hills of South Dakota have gold! Silver is also in the land. Land in other parts of the state has coal, limestone, and gravel.

The **Badlands** have clay, iron, ash, and silt mixed into the land. These things make the hills turn pretty colors in the sunlight!

South Dakota has only a few forests. Most of them are in the Black Hills.

The Badlands in South Dakota.

Beginnings

Native Americans first came to South Dakota about 10,000 years ago. Huge bison, four-horned antelopes, saber-tooth tigers, and other strange animals lived there too. Later, these animals died out, and people hunted buffalo and fished.

From the 1300s through the 1500s, the **Arikara** and the **Cheyenne** lived there. Later, the **Dakota** people came to the area.

By the late 1700s, the Dakota people lived all through South Dakota, North Dakota, Nebraska, and Kansas. They used the Black Hills as a place of worship because it was **sacred** to them.

In the 1800s, traders and settlers came to South Dakota. Many of the settlers were **immigrants**. Then gold was found in the western United States, and more

people came. The **Dakota** people watched others dig gold out of their land and build roads across it.

The Dakota fought back. Chief Red Cloud kept a big part of the state safe. Today, that area is in a **reservation**.

Crazy Horse, Sitting Bull, and Big Foot were other important leaders who fought to keep their land safe. The Dakota people were such an important part of the state that it is named after them.

In 1889, South Dakota became the 40th state. In the 1900s, farmers battled **droughts** and other hardships. In the 1930s, dust storms were so heavy they were called **black blizzards**.

South Dakotans found new ways to manage their farms. They also found new jobs. Today people work in tourism and other areas.

The Crazy Horse monument in South Dakota.

B.C. to 1740s

The First South Dakotans

 8000 B.C.: The first Native Americans live in the area now called South Dakota.

 1400s: The **Arikara** grow corn and squash.

 1700s: The **Dakota** move into South Dakota and rule a large part of the upper Midwest.

 1743: French explorers arrive, the first non-Native American people to come to South Dakota. Trappers begin to hunt and trade furs.

South Dakota

B.C. to 1740s

1850s to 1870s

Golden Lands

1850s-1860s: **Immigrant** farmers move to South Dakota. Gold is found in the western United States.

1868: The Laramie Treaty is signed after two years of war between Red Cloud and the U.S. Army. It says no roads can be built through **sacred** land. The treaty sets up a **reservation**.

1874: Gold is found in South Dakota.

South Dakota

1850s to 1870s

1889 to Today

Hard Times, Better Times

1889: South Dakota becomes the 40th state.

1890: Almost 300 **Dakota** are killed in the Battle of Wounded Knee.

1930s: **Droughts** and dust storms hurt the people and their farms.

1979: The United States government rules that the Black Hills belong to the Dakota Native Americans.

1994: South Dakota corn crops are the best ever.

South Dakota

1889 to Today

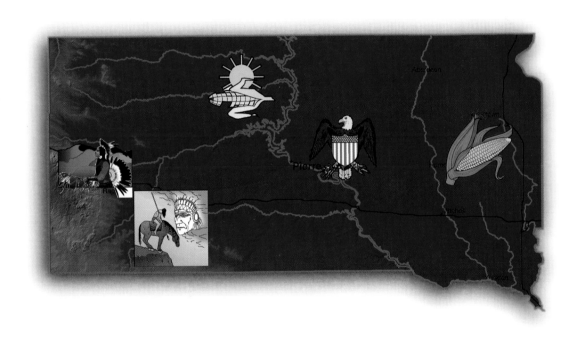

South Dakota's People

There are about 700,000 people in South Dakota. That number might look big, but compared to most states, it is very small.

It would take the people in 10 South Dakotas to match the people in one New Jersey! Yet South Dakota is much bigger than New Jersey—so people have a lot of room in South Dakota! A lot of people live on farms or ranches. Some live on **reservations**.

Sitting Bull was born near Bullhead, South Dakota. He was a **Dakota** leader who fought in the Battle of Little Bighorn. Zitkala-Sa was from the Yankton Reservation. She helped make a law saying Native Americans had the same rights as all United States citizens.

Senators Hubert Humphrey and George McGovern were born in South Dakota. Humphrey also was vice president of the United States.

TV news reporter Tom Brokaw is from Webster, South Dakota. Baseball manager Sparky Anderson was born in Bridgewater, South Dakota. And Billy Mills was born on the Pine Ridge **Reservation** in South Dakota. He was the only person from the United States to win an Olympic gold medal for the 10,000-meter race.

Hubert Humphrey

Sitting Bull

Tom Brokaw

South Dakota's Cities

The largest city in South Dakota is Sioux Falls. Rapid City and Aberdeen are the second and third largest cities. Pierre is the capital of South Dakota.

Deadwood is in the Black Hills. It once was a part of the Wild West. Wild Bill Hickok was killed there.

The city of Lead has a gold mine. It holds more gold than most of the mines in the United States!

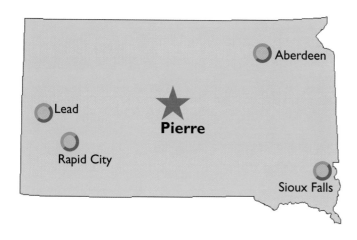

The state capitol building in Pierre, South Dakota.

South Dakota's Land

South Dakota is shaped like a long box dragging a loose ribbon. It is mostly square, but a little piece hangs down in one corner.

South Dakota's land is divided into two regions. The western two thirds is called the Great Plains. In the very western part of this region are steep, rocky hills covered with pine and spruce trees. When you look at them from far away, the trees make them look black. So the **Dakota** Indians called them the Black Hills.

South of the Black Hills are the low, rock-covered **Badlands**.

The region is also covered with treeless

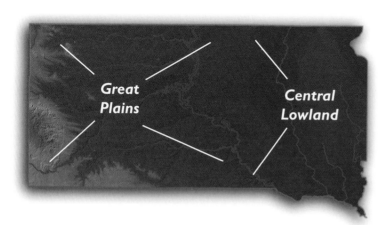

open areas where thousands of sheep and cattle graze.

The other region is called the Central Lowland. This region has rich prairie land. Pasque flowers, black-eyed susans, goldenrods, sunflowers, and poppies grow throughout South Dakota. And cactus grows in the western part of the state!

The Missouri River runs all the way through South Dakota, from the north to the south. To the west is the **Cheyenne** River. To the east is the James River.

The Black Hills in South Dakota.

South Dakotans at Play

    South Dakotans have many parks, lakes, and rivers to enjoy. People from all around America visit Mount Rushmore National Memorial in the Black Hills. Here they can see the faces of presidents George Washington, Thomas Jefferson, Abraham Lincoln, and Theodore Roosevelt carved in the side of a cliff.

    In Mitchell, South Dakota, dances, art shows, and music events are held at the Corn Palace. Also in Mitchell are many paintings by Native Americans at the Oscar Howe Art Center.

    Wild Bill Hickok, Calamity Jane, and other people from the Wild West are buried in Deadwood. The Crazy Horse Memorial near Custer has a big sculpture of the **Dakota** chief.

The Snow Queen Festival is held in Aberdeen every January. In the summer, you can visit the world of Laura Ingalls Wilder at an event in De Smet. And there are rodeo events in many towns like Rapid City.

Sylvan Lake in the Black Hills of South Dakota.

South Dakotans at Work

Many South Dakotans work in places that **tourists** visit. They also work in hospitals and sell things like food or tractors.

Many people are farmers. They grow oats, rye, sunflower seeds, and keep bees that make honey.

South Dakotans also make things. They make foods and farm machines. And many work with jewelry made from the gold in the South Dakota hills.

Opposite page: Many people in South Dakota work on farms.

Fun Facts

•South Dakota and North Dakota were one big area before they became states. Then they were cut into two and made into states at the same time. The president mixed up the papers so no one would ever know which was first to become a state. That way, neither state could say it was more important. Together they were the 39th and the 40th states. Today, we follow the alphabet. Since "N" comes before "S," we say that North Dakota is the 39th state and South Dakota is the 40th.

•The Homestake Mine in Lead, South Dakota, has been working longer than any other mine in the world.

•Calamity Jane pretended to be a soldier when she came to Deadwood, South Dakota in 1875.

•The movie *Dances With Wolves* was filmed in South Dakota.

- There are more than 10,000 duckbilled dinosaurs buried in South Dakota. They died 65 million years ago.
- The biggest herd of buffalo in the world is in Standing Butte Ranch near Pierre.
- Every summer in Sturgis thousands of people ride their motorcycles to one of the biggest rallies in the world.

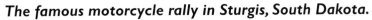

The famous motorcycle rally in Sturgis, South Dakota.

Glossary

Arikara: people who lived in South Dakota long ago; they farmed and traded horses with the Cheyenne.

Badlands: a stretch of land in western South Dakota; the Dakota called them "bad" lands because they were rocky and sometimes hard to travel through, but they are pretty to visit and look at.

Black blizzard: the nickname given to very thick dust storms that came to South Dakota in the 1930s.

Cheyenne: people who lived in South Dakota long ago; they were hunters.

Dakota: people who came to South Dakota in the 1600s; they soon ruled a big area in the northern United States.

Drought: a long period of time with no rain or snow.

Immigrant: a person who comes from another country.

Latino: people who came from Central and South America.

Reservations: an area of land set aside for Native Americans to live on.

Sacred: something that is very important to a group of people, like a church or synagogue; the Black Hills were sacred lands to the Dakota.

Tourist: a person who visits other places for fun.

Internet Sites

The Black Hills, South Dakota
http://www.rapidweb.com/
This site is very colorful and interactive, with web links, arts, outdoors, tours and travel, and many fun things to do in South Dakota.

Gateway to the Black Hills
http://rapidnet.com/~srbrown/rapid.html
This is a very cool site. It has a lot of color and interaction. It's about the Great Sioux Nation, sports, running, biking, hiking, and community. It also has links to places like Field & Stream.

These sites are subject to change. Go to your favorite search engine and type in South Dakota for more sites.

PASS IT ON

Tell Others Something Special About Your State
To educate readers around the country, pass on interesting tips, places to see, history, and little known facts about the state you live in. We want to hear from you!
To get posted on ABDO & Daughters website, e-mail us at "mystate@abdopub.com"

Index